Paris Travel Guide for Women

For Women, by Women: The Insider's Guide to the "City of Lights"

By Erica Stewart

Published by:

ALEX-PUBLISHING

TABLE OF CONTENTS

Author's Note

Welcome to the City of Lights!

The French capital is one city in the world which needs very little introduction. The coveted holiday destination of everyone on the planet, or so it seems, is a powerhouse of amazing enticements. With its stupendous architecture, abundance of art, interesting history, unbelievable shopping and mouth-watering cuisine, Paris is one of those places you could visit once a year every year, until eternity, and still not do it, see it and feast on it all.

The overwhelming variety of attractions and activities make this the foremost destination of, well, just about anyone. Irrespective of age, interests and traveling styles, Paris truly has something to offer everyone. Having said this, Paris is also a particularly fabulous mecca for women travelers: women who love good food, wicked architecture, art, fashion, pampering, history and fun. Whether it's the best wellness spas or flea markets you wish to discover, or organized tours, nighttime activities and delectable street food, we've got Paris wrapped up in a nutshell.

Best,

Erica Stewart

Chapter 1: What to Know Before You Go

Best time to visit – Paris is a phenomenal place to visit no matter the time of year but, naturally, there are a few months which are simply ideal. March, April and May (Spring) are superb: the bitter chill of winter is gone and it's not yet so hot that you risk heat exhaustion as

you spend your days sightseeing. Moreover, flowerbeds in all the fabulous parks will be in full bloom, and the whole city will be just bursting with vibrant color and activities. If you can, avoid July and August like the plague. The European summer attracts literally millions of foreign tourists, making attractions overcrowded, and everything closes down for a few weeks in August anyway. Travel here at this time and you'll b sharing the Paris with a gazillion tourists, who'll be just as frustrated as you are that everything's closed. Not much fun. Do note that a winter visit is actually quite special, despite the bitter cold. The lack of masses and startling beauty of a city wrapped in a winter fog is simply spectacular.

City Orientation – Paris is made up of 20 suburbs called "arrondissements". They are numbered – starting with 1 in the immediate historic city centre (Notre Dame Cathedral) – and spread out on a clockwise-spiral, so 1 is bordered (from north, to north-east, south etc) by 2, 3, 4, 5, 6, 7 and 8. For tourists, the most popular hoods are any from 1 to 9, as well as 18, Montmartre. Do note that even at its furthest point (18 and 20), you can be in the city centre in under 20 minutes by underground Metro. Arrondissements are detailed in the next chapter.

All hail the Metro - Paris has one of the most comprehensive and insanely convenient underground train systems of any European cities. There's a station every few blocks, all over the city, and trains run every 2-3 minutes. Plus, it's super affordable! This is arguably one of the best things Paris has going for it, as far as logistics is concerned. Sure, it lacks the 'clean, sterile, air-conditioned feel of the German Bahn, but boy is it amazing. Most visitors find themselves taking at least 5

Metro rides every day they are in Paris, due to the sheer convenience and speediness of it all. Do note, that the Metro closes at either 1 am or 2 am (weekdays and weekend) and starts again at 5.30 am. For solo female travelers, the best option during these closures are taxi, but they are quite expensive at night. You'll find plenty more transport info in the 'How to Get Around' chapter.

Where to stay – thanks to the Metro, you can opt to skip the super expensive accommodation in the city centre and can choose to stay a little further out of town. However, when choosing your hotel/hostel/B&B, make sure you'll be within *very* close walking distance to a metro stop (5 mins max) and, for even more convenience, that it's on a direct line to the '1e arrondissement' (ie. you need not switch line half way through your journey). Having said all this...if you're the kind of woman who loves to go on a shopping spree, loves an after-lunch siesta, afternoon shower and three clothing changes a day, then staying closes to the 'action' may be a wiser choice. A 20-minute Metro ride is a piece of cake when you're only doing it two times a day, not four.

Prioritize – The idea of visiting Paris once a year every year, to all eternity, is incredibly romantic. Albeit probably not very realistic. When visiting Paris, it pays to prioritize your interests and even (shock horror!) make a list of everything you'd like to see and do. Then, cull it. Thinking you'll be able to see and do it all on a single visit is lunacy and, considering many people don't account for museum queues, travel times and tiredness, many a first-time traveler has left Paris with a distinctive feeling of disappointment., Don't be that gal. be the gal who knows what she wants, can't be brutally selective and leaves plenty of time to just *be*, in Paris. Walks along the Seine, leisurely lunches and infinite café stops in Paris, can be as rewarding as visiting the Louvre or climbing the Eiffel Tower. Keep that in mind.

The Eiffel Tower conundrum – Speaking of the Eiffel Tower...There are a few tall, man-made structures the world over that are simply amazing to admire with your own eyes. The Eiffel Tower is one such treasure. But, the highlighting here is the tower itself, meaning that if you wish to save yourself the time, stress and expense of actually climbing it, know that you won't be missing out on a truly magical experience. It's not. Admire it from below, or from the top of the Montmartre Hill, and enjoy it in all its glory. This is the most iconic and resplendent of Paris' landmarks. Once you can no longer see it – because you are on top of it - the city skyline can appear quite ordinary. We've just saved you at least three hours of your Paris holiday time. You're welcome!

As for the Versailles Palace... – Along a similar line of thought, the Palace of Versailles is an inherently historical treasure in France and can be said to be where the modern-day country spawned. Yet making the effort to visit it should probably be reserved for history buffs primarily, considering admission cost is expensive, the line to get in can be horrendous. Moreover, unless you go on a splendidly sunny Spring day (to enjoy the amazing gardens and fountains – which you can do for free), it may not seem all that impressive. As much as it pains us to admit it, taking up a whole day to travel and visit the Versailles is only really worth it IF you have AT LEAST a whole week at your disposal. Ouch. There. We said it.

Sail the Seine – Overdone and over-touristy it may be, but taking a trip down the Seine on the Bateaux-Mouches is anything but overrated. Paris is utterly gorgeous from the water, as many of its priceless buildings were built right on the shore. Don't miss you chance to take a cruise along the Seine, it will be one of the many highlights of your visit, we assure you.

Give the Louvre the respect it deserves – Believe it or not, there's more to the Louvre than a 10-second peek at the miniscule Mona Lisa hiding hanging behind a bulletproof glass. This is one of the world's foremost art museums and, once you've lined up for an hour and paid a fair price to get in, don't just visit Lisa and walk out. The Louvre deserves at least 4 hours of your time, as it is home to the some of the most priceless artwork the world has ever seen. Between the paintings and sculptures you'll be utterly overwhelmed by the beauty of this place, so plan plenty of time to appreciate it in full.

Learn the basics – Parisians have a (somewhat) bad reputation for being particularly unfriendly to English-speaking visitors. They're not. Well, they are, sort of. They do tend to get a bit narky with tourists who seem to make no effort whatsoever to at least *greet* them in French. Learn the basic greetings and bring a long an English-French dictionary, especially if you choose not to stay in the immediate city centre. You'll need it.

Choose comfort over elegance – Watch any movie filmed in Paris and you may come to the erroneous conclusion that all Parisian women wear vertiginous heels on a daily basis, and dress to impress *all* the time. Although they may do this to dine out, mostly they wear jeans, trainers (perhaps not white ones) all sorts of comfy shoes and plain cotton Ts. Pack comfortable clothing for your days out exploring the city, and include one dressy outfit for a night out in town. Whatever you do, however, do not bring half a dozen scarves nor any kind of beret. In Paris, that's the easiest way to pick a tourist.

Be alert in scamville – From the passerby who just miraculously found a silver ring and wants you to have it (for a couple of Euros, perhaps?) to the pretend-adeaf woman who'll put a friendship bracelet on your wrist or the shoe shiner who tries to engage you while his friend pickpockets you, Paris is the city of ingenuous scams. Be alert around the tourist sites but chill out everywhere else. Unlike other major European capitals, like Rome, Munich or Vienna, Paris doesn't shut down on Sundays. Yey!

Adapt...your gadgets – Universal adaptor plugs are particularly difficult to find in Paris, so avoid the hassle of hunting one down and pack one from home. France runs on 220 volts, so check to see the voltage requirement for all your gadgets (including that travel hairdryer!) as you may also need to pack a travel-converter.

Be free – Paris is renowned as an expensive city, yet the sheer amount of absolutely free delights actually makes it one of the most affordable. From picnics to parks, outdoor markets and free-to-enter churches, one could seriously spend a whole week here and spend very little.

Chapter 2: Getting in & General Overview

Paris, the most visited city on the planet, is comprehensively serviced by three major airports, the largest of which is the Charles de Gaulle International Airport, and extensive rail and bus terminals. Prices for transport to/from varies depending on which day/time you are travelling, so check online with the supplied websites before you travel.

GET IN BY AIR

What: Charles de Gaulle International Airport – the main aviation hub

Where: 31kms (19 miles) north-east of the city centre

City Transfers: **By Train** The RER commuter train stops in both T3 and T2. If you arrive/leave from T1, you can reach T3 via the free airport terminal shuttle. You can buy your train ticket directly at the terminal. Look out for 'All trains to Paris' sign; expect the ride to take about 40 minutes. This is the fastest way to reach Paris' city centre from the airport. The train will take you to the city's northern train terminal. From here you can reach all corners of the city.

By Bus Catch the <u>Roissy Bus</u> service from any of the terminals, which will take you to the Opera Garnier building in central Paris. Due to the high volume of traffic, however, this trip can take an hour and a half, or even more. <u>AirFrance</u> also runs frequent buses to and from Montparnase (14e arrondissement).

Shared shuttle the convenient <u>shared shuttle service</u> is a great compromise between public and private transport, (door to door service) but you still have to account for traffic congestion.

Taxis Are expensive but very convenient, obviously. A ride into the city should never cost more than €150, but can be had for as little as €50, which is great if shared with three travel companions. Pre-book your safe and reliable taxi service right <u>here</u>.

Special note: The airport comprises three large terminals which are quite away from each other, so transfers to gates often require (free) 15-min shuttle transport. Leave yourself plenty of time when leaving the country and account for it when arriving.

What: <u>Orly International Airport</u> – mostly used by Air France and European carriers

Where: About 18kms (11 miles) south of Paris' city centre.

City Transfers: **By Train** The <u>RER</u> runs a southern line which connects passengers to the city centre.

By Bus The <u>OrlyBus</u> service will take you to/from the Metro station at Denfert-Rochereau in about 30 minutes or so. When leaving, head to the southern Orly Metro station and head to Platform 4.

By Taxi Cabs are available directly outside the terminal, expect the cost to be about €50. Or, you can pre-book one online <u>here</u>.

What: Beauvais Airport – The hub of European low-cost carriers

Where: 89 kms (55 miles) south-east of Paris' city centre

City Transfers: **By Train** The <u>TER (regional line)</u> will have you to/from the airport in under an hour and a half, but you will have to transfer in Beauvais city centre, about 3.5km from the airport, as the aviation hub as no direct rail connection. A shuttle runs between Tille and the airport, or you can also grab a cab. The train from the airport arrives at Gare du Nord in Paris.

By Bus Buses run from the Beauvais Airport to the Paris Congress Centre, nearby the Porte Maillot RER station, from where you can connect to the Paris Metro service. Buy your bus ticket directly at the Arrivals Terminal.

GET IN BY TRAIN

Perhaps unsurprisingly, considering the city grew exponentially over a short period of time, Paris lacks one major, central railway station. Instead the city is home to half a dozen prominent hubs, in its opposing ends, which are not even directly linked.

They are:

- Gare d'Austerlitz – 13th arrondissement: For services to central and southern France, and Spain

- Gare de l'Est - 10th arrondissement: To southern Germany

- Gare de Lyon – 12th arrondissement: To the Southern Alps and over to Italy

- Gare Montparnasse – 14th arrondissement: To the south west of France and Burgundy region

- Gare du Nord – 10th arrondissement: Services the Eurostar to Belgium and Holland

- Gare St Lazare – 8th arrondissement: Services to Normandy

For detailed timetables and to book your tickets in or out of Paris by train, refer to the official SNCF Website

OVERVIEW OF PARIS AND ITS ARRONDISSEMENTS

No matter how overwhelming Paris may seem at first, to the uninitiated, it is a remarkably easy city to navigate. It takes merely a full-day out sightseeing to build a mental picture of the layout of the city and location of all the arrondissements, especially as to how they relate to one another.

Here's a brief outline of Paris' arrondissements, and what they each have to offer:

1st – The heart and core of the city, here you'll find Notre Dame, the Louvre, the northern bank of the Seine (sightseeing boats for cruises), the Arc de Triomphe, Place de la Concord, the Champs Elysees and a myriad of museums and points of interest. The bulk of your sightseeing will arguably be done here.

2nd – The National Library, Paris stock exchange and main commercial hub is locate here, just a couple of kms north of the city centre. Perhaps not so many individual POIs but amazing architecture and amazing historic shopping arcades.

3rd – The Old Jewish Quarter with a plethora of traditional houses, amazing ethnic foods and trendy little shops. The medieval core of La Marais is here, as well as the interesting Jewish History Museum.

4th – This trendy-bohemian hood is awash with designer, one-of-a-kind boutiques, brilliant street art and a variety of trendy B&Bs.

5th – The 'Left bank' of the Seine is Paris' Latin Quarter, this is the oldest 'suburb' in the city, built by the Romans almost 2,000 years ago. Fantastic Roman ruins and superlative Islam Mosques are found here.

6th – Where all the famous artistic and intellectual revolutionaries used to converge to moan and groan about the French aristocracy, the 6th arrondissement is nowadays one of Paris' trendiest hoods. Here you'll find amazing churches and stunning bridges.

7th – Home of the Eiffel Tower, this is one of Paris' greenest and most visited suburbs (obviously), also boasting some amazing museums. Ironically, not the most 'exciting' arrondissement to stay in.

8th – Designer gear and luxurious opulence denotes this arrondissement, which shares the Arc de Triomphe and Champs Elysees with the 1st.

9th – The Opera Garnier and two major department stores (Printemps and Galerie La Fayette), this arrondissement is exceptionally popular with shoppers.

10th – The lovely Canal St Martin gifts this suburb a very leafy and relaxing atmosphere. Being home to two major train terminals also makes it a popular choice with many visitors.

11th – This is the young, hip, happening and rebellious suburb, chock-full of students, struggling artists and wicked nightclubs.

12th – A 'family friendly' hood with big, open, green spaces, historic squares and a lot of shopping and dining options.

13th – Perhaps the most overlooked of all, the 13th arrondissement is the closest thing to Chinatown as one can get in Paris. If you want authentic and ethnic Parisian, minus the romantic tourist fluff, then you'd love it to bits.

14th – We swing back into the touristy side, with a suburb home to the famed Boulevard de Montparnasse and Paris Catacombs.

15th – Probably the least charming suburb in the city, full of 1970s apartment buildings which have garnered quite the abysmal reputation among the trendy Parisians.

16th – the French Open tennis tournament at Roland Garros is held in this suburb, one of the most fashionable and up market in Paris. Lots of grand mansions and plenty of museums here.

17th – This is one of Paris' most up and coming hoods, which means it's trendy yet still very affordable.

18th – One of the most exciting hoods of all, with the stunning Sacre Coeur Church and Moulin Rouge theatre at its core. Fantastic to explore at length (SO many trendy laneways) but perhaps not the safest hood for a lone female traveler, no matter how adventurous!

19th & 20th – The outer suburbs of Paris are excellent for their green open spaces and authentic everything. But they are quite out of town and, if it's your first time in Paris, may not be the most ideal choice.

Chapter 3: How to Get Around

Paris is one of the easiest major world capitals in which to get around. Compared to many other cities, the public transport is fantastic and, once in you're in an arrondissement of interest, you'll want to do nothing else but walk. Paris, on foot, is just priceless. The architecture, small hidden shops, plethora of cool trendy little cafés and iconic street scenes means that you never want Paris to just 'fly by'. You want to savor each and every step.

Use a combination of the following and you'll have Paris wrapped around your little finger in no time.

Metro & RER

At the risk of sounding repetitive: the Paris Metro is amazing! The city is traversed by more than 300kms of train tracks, and dotted with over 300 stations. No matter where you need to go, you'll find a Metro stop, at most, only two blocks away. The RER (regional train service) shares many of the lines of the Metro and, for all intents and purposes, it makes no difference to you which one you take. There are 16 lines in total, and services run from 5 am until 12.30 am. Never bother to 'check for times', simply show up and catch the next train. In peak hour they come along every 2 minutes, and off-peak they run about 5-7 minutes apart.

A single ticket is valid for travel between destinations, with as many line changes as necessary, within a 2-hour period. Although tickets are inexpensive (€1.80 at time of print), most visitors find themselves taking anywhere between three and seven roes a day. It can add up. Purchase a multi-day ParisVisite Card which includes unlimited travel for either 1, 2, 3 or 5 days. You can choose how many zones to include (1, 2, 3 or 5) and frugal travelers may want to note that it is absolutely not worth it, for the price, to include all 5 zones. This is what you would need to get back to the airport when you leave, but a single fare to the airport, on your last day, will be much cheaper than the price ticket of the more comprehensive tourist pass. When venturing out to outer attractions like the Bastille or Disneyland, it pays to buy a separate, one off ticket on the day you travel.

Some tips to keep in mind:

- Metro stations are amazing points of orientation, should you ever get lost. There is one every few blocks along the major artery of any arrondissement, and they all display an extensive map of the nearby area downstairs.

- Once you've worked which station you wish to reach, simply look to see what line it's on (on this handy Metro map) note the last station on that line in the direction in which you wish to travel. Once at the station, look for trains directed towards that last station. Trains stop at all stations.

- Not all train doors open automatically so, if you are the first in line to alight the train, press the lever (sometimes the button) to open the door once the train has come to a stop.

Buses

Paris' extensive albeit confusing bus system is best left for those rare instances when the Metro doesn't get you close enough to your intended destination. On the upside, although figuring out which bus to take may be a hassle, once you are *on* the bus, it's a breeze! Your Metro ticket is valid for the ride and displays inside the bus point out exactly where you are, what the ext station is and all subsequent stops. In this regard, it is very tourist-friendly. Bus maps are available at every major Metro station.

Bicycles

An ever growing trend among foreign tourists, cycling around Paris is the fave mode to get around for many

Parisians. The city boasts a great bike share program, called the Vélib', which is both inexpensive and very comprehensive. Stations are scattered around town and, considering Paris is already a bike-friendly city, this makes for a great (and healthy!) alternative to the buses and trains. Imagine how many more éclairs you could devour?!

Chapter 4: Top 10 Iconic Paris Experiences

Paris offers an infinite number of outstanding experiences, and this holds true whether you're here for the first time or the 100th, in company or flying solo. Paris may be renowned as the world's most romantic city, but it doesn't mean that a solo female traveler will not have an absolute blast here. In fact, much like New York, Paris is simply ideal for solo women adventurers. The city is as safe as it is fascinating and, because it has SO much to offer, travelling solo means you need not waste time compromising and doing something to please a travel partner. Paris...is all about you!

If you think you'll be visiting a lot of attractions and museums, then check out the Paris Museum Pass, available for two, four and six days. Alternatively, opt for the Paris Pass, for and unlimited public transport access plus a host of discounts and queue-jumping benefits to dozens of attractions.

Here are just some of the most incredible things you can see and do:

Join an organized tour

Even if you're a seasoned solo female traveler, with a wealth of knowledge and experience behind you, you'll gain a heck of a lot of insight – and have a lot of fun – by joining one of the city's excellent walking tours. Let a local, knowledgeable and enthusiastic young guide show you around, impart loads of fascinating info and help you get to grips with the most historic part of town. WEGO Tours are one of the best rated companies in Paris and offer very comprehensive and super fun walking tours of the 1st District. If you have a bit of excess energy to burn on your first day, then you can see Paris on two wheels with Blue Bike Tours or join one the extremely popular Segway Tours. Doing this on your first day in Paris will build your confidence and prove to you just how compact and easy to handle this metropolis really is.

Tick off the Holy Trinity of Paris sightseeing

The Eiffel Tower, the Notre Dame Cathedral and the Louvre Museum. Admire the first from every which angle and spend hours taking selfies to your heart's delight, climb the tower of the second to absorb the utterly breathtaking views....and spend hours admiring the priceless artwork of the last. Done. Whether or not you're religious, appreciate architecture or art is almost irrelevant here: you just can't come to Paris and not visit the city's three most revered and celebrated treasures.

Sail the Seine

Admiring Paris while cruising the Seine is not just iconic: it's an absolutely unmissable experience. You will enjoy the most stunning side of the French capital, whether on a 2 or 4-hour long sightseeing trip, champagne and canapés cruise or full three-course dinner cruise with world-famous Bateaux Mouches. If you're short on time, then hop on the Batobus, the ferry service which runs through the heart of Paris, stops at 9 strategic locations and is a brilliant way to get to other attractions and enjoy a cruise down the Seine. Buy your full-day ticket here.

Don't miss the **Musée d'Orsay**

Built as a train station in the late 19th century, and showed off at 1900 World Fair, the Musée d'Orsay is as revered for its contents as for its exquisite exterior. Boasting the largest collection of French impressionist art in the world, it is a mecca for art and architecture lovers. With works by Gaugain, Van Gogh, Monet, Manet (among so many more), a stunning restaurant, breathtaking glassed roof and two trendy cafés, a visit here can even surpass the Louvre. To appreciate it, you'll need to set aside at least three hours of your day.

Spend a day wondering the streets of Le Marais

Often rated as Paris' foremost hub, Le Marais takes up chunks of both the 3rd and 4th districts and is awash with spectacular museums (like the Carnavalet and Picasso), the historic Jewish Quarter, a myriad of super trendy cafés and restaurants and more gorgeous boutiques than you could wave a MasterCard to. Le Marais was one of Paris' most aristocratic suburbs and boasts stunning mansions and buildings lining charming cobblestone alleyways.

Retreat to the quiet sanctuaries of Paris' regal gardens

The Palais Royal is a striking 17th century palace-turned-museum across the Louvre on Rue de Montpensier and it boasts one of the city's most hidden treasures: the manicured Royal Palace gardens. Finding a quiet place to retreat to, right in the heart of the bustling city, is heavenly. Recently restored to their glory, the gardens are an ideal place to head to on a gloriously sunny day, especially if armed with a picnic basket of cheeses, hams and a little bottle of red. A few designer clothing, perfume and antique boutiques add a real touch of exclusivity to this place. If you're around the 6th arrondissement, then you can find your reprieve in the magical gardens of the Luxembourg Palace, which were created by order of Queen Marie de Medici in the early 1600s. The Jardin du Luxembourg is home to a former royal Orangerie, pavilions, over 100 statues and a myriad of exotic flower beds.

Stroll down the Champs Elysees

Even if you can't stretch your holiday budget enough to actually *buy* something from the designer boutiques along the world's most famous shopping avenue, you've still got to see it! From the Arc de Triomphe to Egyptian Obelisk, this stretch of the Champs Elysees houses more exclusive boutiques than you'd find anywhere else. Nowadays, it also houses some dubious international department-store like brands and the whole place attracts the largest crowds in the city. But...the tree lined avenue, which is simply superb in spring and summer, and also boasts plenty of cafés, ideal if you want to stretch your stroll to a few hours.

Take in the views from the Sacre Coeur Basilica

Montmartre most famous attractions is the splendid church of Sacre Coeur, built in 1914 atop a 130m hill, one of the city's highest. Its impressive architecture, and the sweeping city views its location grants, make this one of Paris' most popular attraction, helped by the fact that it's found in one of the city's most eclectic arrondissements. While it used to be home to struggling artists and rebellious intellectuals, this suburb is not of the most coveted in the city and attracts arguably the largest tourist crowds of all, making it now also one of the most expensive. You'll find an array of charming boutiques and bakeries, a sleuth of street art and a vibrant and very social scene here.

Savor an ice cream at Berthillon

The Maison Berthillon is the most famous – and oldest - ice cream parlor in Paris and, although many of the city's top restaurants purchase their delectably creamy dessert from here, savoring your own coney delight at the source is purely epic. Found in the heart of Ile St Louis (that little island in the heart of the Seine), Berthillon is revered for the creaminess of their ice cream and amazing flavor selections. Go salted butter caramel or chocolate fondant, and you'll never think of ice cream the same way again. As you walk towards the café, you'll see many others offering original Berthillon ice cream, so do make sure you do find the right one.

Learn to cook French food like a pro

French cuisine has a long and illustrious history and is renowned as a complex, decadent and even fastidious fare. Learn to cook a meal fit for kings and queens and spend a few hours in the company of fun, ravenous chefs who love nothing more than to share the secrets of their passion with. Particularly ideal for solo female travelers, the classes held by Cook'n With Class are absolute Paris highlight and rated as the best in the city. Run by an American chef with insider know-how, the classes are varied, insightful, delicious and always entertaining. Master the art of produce market shopping, baking delights and pairing meals with wine.

Chapter 5: Girl's Day Out in Paris

From shopping galore to spa treatments and more chocolate than you could ever wish for, enjoying girly days in Paris is truly effortless.

Here are just some of the fun stuff you can do in Paris, whether travelling alone or with friends!

Splurge on shoes and underwear - Never have two items of clothing and accessories been more suited to each other than classy shoes and sexy underwear. Shop for both along Rue de Cherche-Midi, a long and illustrious avenue chock full of the most divine shoe and intimate apparel shops. The fact it is also brimming with delectable bakeries should not go unnoticed.

Opera Garnier – Get dolled up and spend a night at the opera with your besties, where you can sip champagne, watch a show and enjoy being in one of the most luxurious theatres in the world.

Relax in a hammam – Soaking in the therapeutic steam of a Turkish bath-house is one of the most delightful ways to rest and unwind, especially on the last day of your Paris trip. Soak for a while, then let one of the ladies scrub and massage you into a blissful state of relaxation. The most popular hammams are at the Mosquee de Paris, and Le Bains du Marais.

Catch the Parish Fashion Week – Spring in Paris is all about high fashion, and if you travel here in March you can score tickets to one of the world's most respected fashion paardes. Because nothings 'This gal has been to Paris' like a stub from a ticket to a designer fashion show!

Catch a fashion show...anytime! – can't make it to Paris for THE fashion show? Never mind! Head to the Galleries Lafayette in Fridays and Saturdays during high summer season, and you can score a (Free!) ticket to one of their many fabulous in-house shows.

Indulge in a hot chocolate at Angelina's – The British may do 'a spot of afternoon tea', yet the French swoon for a cup of hot chocolate at this Parisian institution. One of the most famous and decadent coffee houses in Paris, Angelina's is an absolute delight for all the senses.

Decorate your life– If you love anything to do with interior design and décor, and are travelling to Paris in January, then don't miss the Masion & Object Fair where you can be privy to some of the outstanding and delightful home décor ideas you'll probably ever see outside a catalogue.

While away a few hours at <u>Shakespear and Co</u> – writers, readers and book aficionados love to retreat to this little haven in the 5th arrondissement. If you're a lover of the old-school literary world then you're bound to fall in complete awe of this place. With the addition of a new café, this place is bound to gain an even bigger cult following.

Spend a morning on Place des Vosges – One of the oldest in Paris, this historic, elegant and utterly charming square delineates the 3rd and 4th arrondissements and is a beautiful place in which to spend a relaxing morning. Place des Vosges is Europe's first square, built in the 17th century, after which all others were modeled. One home to some of the most illustrious members of the French aristocracy, it is nowadays a wonderful place in which to socialize, museum-hop, shop and dine.

Enjoy a full day of fitness – need a full day off sightseeing? Then indulge in a gorgeous day at the <u>Ritz Hotel</u> Health Club where a day-pass grants you access to the gym, pool, sauna, hammam, Jacuzzi and fitness classes.

Chapter 6: Feast Like a Local

After the sightseeing, museum-hopping, hammam-indulging and shopping, you'll have only one thing left to do: eat your way through Paris. This, as you may imagine, is much easier than you ever thought possible. Paris is home to over 60 Michelin-starred restaurants and, when it comes to haute-cuisines, there are few world capitals which can hope to compete. Yet Paris and its phenomenal foodie scene is so much more than posh dinners in ridiculously expensive establishments frequented by the world's rich and famous. It's about crusty warm baguettes bought from hole-in-the-wall bakeries, about finding that hidden deli brimming with 101 types of cheeses. It's about packing a picnic basket and heading to a suburban garden, about spending hours trying the treats in a local, unknown market and understanding that gorging on a kebab on the side of the road, is as iconic as it gets, in Paris.

Food, glorious food. In Paris...it's everywhere.

The best way to stumble upon that excellent little local place is to stumble upon it, by accident. As long as you steer clear of overly touristy blocks, you'll find appetizing food all over this big, tasty metropolis. So instead, we'll help you out with some local, insider tips for locating the most hidden delectable spots of all.

PRODUCE MARKETS

Holiday rental apartments are insanely popular in Paris and much of this has to do with the city's array of amazing fresh produce markets. The days of buying vegetables, meat, fish, cheese and fruit from local farmers markets may be a thing of the past in many countries, but in France this cultural habit is still very much alive. Every arrondissement has its own produce market, held on a particular day of the week. You just have to know where to go! Your local land-lady, or hotel concierge, is the best person to advise you as to the closest market. No matter which one you choose to visit, keep in mind that you should aim to get there no later than 10 am.

These, are the most famous and best stocked:

Marche Bastille, Bastille – On boulevard Richard Lenoir, this bi-weekly market is overflowing with organic fresh produce, and a lot of stupendous foreign wares and food from Northern Africa and beyond. A true feast for all the senses. Thursdays and Sundays.

Marche Mouffetard, 5th arrondissement – Ernest Hemingway once described this compact marketplace as a 'movable feast' and he was certainly not wrong.

Here, you'll find the best of the organic and fair-trade produce, and a host of scrumptious pastries, pâtés and cured meats. Every day except Mondays.

Marche Monger – In the Latin Quarter you'll find this posh-looking market which tends to be more expensive than the others, yet also carries the crème-de-la-crème of fresh produce. Believe that you get what you pay for, and simply want the best? Shop here.

Marche International de Rungis – A visit here, not unlike one at the Louvre, should be confronted with military precision. This is, after all, the world's largest fresh produce market! It may be a little out of the centre, but once you see it, smell it and taste it, you'll understand why every chef in town gets his/her produce from here. Open every day except Sundays.

Rue Montorgueil, 2nd arrondissement – this hybrid market-food shops haven is a perfect fusion for any food-lover. Shop, eat, shop, eat, repeat. Hip and happening every day of the week, except Monday.

Marche Raspail, 6th arrondissement– this one has it all: a vibrant atmosphere, fantastic produce and amazing array of ready-made treats. What more could one want? Tuesdays, Fridays and Sundays.

STREET FOOD

If you're the kind of woman who's always on the go and prefers not to waste time on long, lingering lunches, then Paris' street food scene is bound to tickle all the right taste buds. It's worthwhile to keep in mind, however, that this is not New York. This is Paris. So even fast made street food grants a sensational and opulent culinary experience.

Here are our favorite haunts:

Chez Aline – Until just a few years ago, the only on-the-go food you could grab on a Parisian side walk was a melt-in-your-mouth, ham-filled baguette. Go straight to the classic source and get your fill at the city's most famous 'ham sandwich spot'. The baguettes at Aline's are second to none, with the purveyor carrying some of the best ham, butter and bread on the whole country. Plenty of other fillings also on offer and a wide array of salads too. You'll find this small deli on 85, Rue de la Roquette, 11th arrondissement.

Frenchie to go – The pastrami sandwiches made by Frenchie are set to rival any found in New York. Don't believe us? Try them! With pastrami, pulled pork and crispy fries on their super-fast, take out menu, Frenchies is reason enough to move to Paris, permanently. Frenchie to Go is on 9, rue du Nil, 2nd arrondissement.

L'Avant Comptoir – When those sweet cravings hit, head to L'Avant Comptoir and dig into the most delectable chocolate and cinnamon crêpe. Take just one bite, and you'll understand the queue. You'll find this stand on 9, Carrefourde l'Odeon, 6th arrondissement.

Grille – There are very few fast-food outlets which can turn a humble 'kebab' into a gastronomic experience. Thanks to the premium home-made meat, and pita bread, grille manages to do just that. For the most scrumptious kebab you'll probably ever have, head to 15, Rue St Augustin in the 2nd arrondissement.

Le Camion Qui Fume –if you're in Paris for a few days, and find yourself starting to miss a good ol' fashion gourmet burger, then make a beeline for this most celebrated food-truck. Run by an American and hailed as the first 'real food truck in Paris', Le Camion location is confirmed daily on their Facebook page.

Cantine California – another American is the brains, and cooking skills, behind Paris' first Tex-Mex food truck, which serves up totally outlandish blue cheese burgers, tacos and chipotle. Check out the website for daily locations.

L'As du Fallafel - Right in the heart of the Jewish Quarter, on 34, Rue des Rosiers, is where you'll find this highly rated Kosher fallafel joint, considered the best Middle Eastern street food in Paris. Or a few Euros, you get piping hot fallafels on a pita bread, topped with grilled aubergine, hummus, tahini, garlic and chili sauce.

Need we say more?

MUST EATS

Every city has its own long list of specialties which may be found in other parts of the world, but are best savored in their original birthplace. And so it is with Paris, only *here* the list is near infinite!

The French don't eat much in the morning. In fact, they don't eat much at all…at least, not all in one sitting. Unlike in most Anglo-Saxon countries, French culture abides by the 'eat small but often' credo and this certainly works in their favor, considering obesity is definitely not a problem in this country. Following the locals' way will have insanely great benefits for you. First of all, you can savor many different local treats in a single day and, secondly, you'll actually save quite a bit of holiday cash, eating small but often.

Here are some of the treats you simply must try whilst in Paris:

Croissants – Light, fluffy, melt-in-your-mouth croissants are *de rigeur* in the morning. Along with a strong cup of coffee, this makes for an authentic Parisian breakfast. Typically, only a light croissant or one of its many variants (see below) is what's consumed for breakfast. But you know what? You're on vacation. You want to have a huge filled profiterole for breakfast? You go girl!

Pain au chocolat – The chocolate croissants is one of the most beloved exports to have come out of Paris. Do yourself a huge favor and, for once, taste them the way they are meant to be.

Éclair – It is possible to revolve your entire vacation around finding THE best éclair in Paris. It's been done before, it can be done again. Over and over again, in fact.

Crêpes – Steer well clear of the pre-made crêpe stands near the Eiffel Tower and you're already a step ahead. For the best crepes, and if you want to eat them on the go, look out for local restaurants with a take-away window on the side. The favored kind in Paris? Ham and cheese of course!

Profiteroles – Parisians tend to gobble down these cream filled, chocolate covered puffs of God only seldom, and even then, won't have more than one. Amateurs. Show them how it's done.

Croque Monsieur/Madame – Lovers of grilled cheese, ham and egg sandwich unite, for here we have the model by which all others should be rated. In this particular case, we do urge you to pick a cozy café and make it a sit-down affair. The Croque deserves your undivided attention.

Quiche Lorraine – This is perhaps the most famous quiche variant to have come out of Paris, although you'll find dozens of different types offered here. Try one, try them all.

Steak Tartare – This 'raw' beef dish is actually delectable, just as soon as you get over the fact you are eating raw meat. Sliced thinly and marinated in alcohol, which cooks it somewhat, this is the French equivalent of the Italian carpaccio.

Onion Soup – You know the world-famous 'French onion soup' seen in menus all over the world? Well, in Paris, for obvious reasons, they drop the French from the name. Still delicious!

Moules – You'll know when black mussels are in season because you'll see the word 'moules' scribbled on restaurant blackboards all over Paris. Baked in a cream and white wine sauce (mouclade), they are simply divine. If you're lucky enough to be travelling in moules season, don't miss them!

Carrefour – Nope, this is not a dish, but a rather famous supermarket, one which you should seek out if you're exhausted from your day's outing and just wish to grab something quick and easy. In Carrefour, even that something quick and easy can be outstanding. You'll find crusty baguettes in the bakery section and a mind-boggling selection of fromages (cheeses!), hams, pates and marinated olives in their deli selections. You know how we said everyone in Paris only ever shops in local produce markets? Well, we lied. Hard working Parisians don't have a lot of time for that kind of romantic shopping trip, and head to Carrefour instead for their weekly grocery shop, leaving only meat and fish for the markets. Carrefour and many other supermarkets (like **Auchan, Intermarche, Franprix and E.Leclerc** among others) are open till late and found in every arrondissement, all over the city. Locate the closest one to your hotel as soon as you arrive, and you'll be all set.

Chapter 7: Shop 'Till You Drop

Shopping is synonymous with Paris although even the most ardent shopaholic may want to rein in their obsession just a tad, when they visit. Aside the fact that Paris is not a cheap place to shop, much of what you'll find here, you will also find at home, and with so many stunning places to see, experiences to make and food to eat, you may not want to spend hours on end lost in one of the many department stores here. What is quite incredible is spending hours perusing the very unique boutiques of most suburbs, discovering flea markets and buying those treats are not found anywhere else. We don't mean berets or scarves, by the way!

Here are the best shopping haunts in Paris:

Le Marais, 3rd & 4th arrondissement - Paris' answer to SoHo, Le Marais is chock-full of hippy, trendy, artisan boutiques selling one offs and very eclectic wares. This is one of the most popular shopping haunts, so do expect it to be crowded and filled with tourists, as well as locals. Discover antiques and artwork, among clothing and homewares, for a truly comprehensive shopping experience.

Charonne, 11th arrondissement – Rue de Charonne near Place de Bastille is one of those shopping strips revered by locals and mostly unknown to visitors. Reason enough to head here? You bet! Quirky, cool yet affordable shopping is what this avenue offers, and it exudes more Parisian charm than most others, combined. Those who do stumble here (mostly by chance) will no doubt wonder if this is the true, last 'village' in Paris. It may well be.

Canal St Martin, 10th arrondissement - Just south of the Place de La Bastille, and stretching out almost all the way to the Seine, the over 4km-long Canal St Martin is mostly renowned for its chic cafés and tree-lined riverside promenade, yet among all this loveliness hide quite a few gorgeous independent boutiques, well worth checking out.

Saint Ouen Flea Market, 18th arrondissement – The world's largest flea market requires patience and endurance. At first, all you see is knock-off cheap sunnies and ghastly clothing, yet if you hang around a little longer, and scour wider, you'll realize why the Saint Ouen market is as popular as it is. Amazing antiques and great second-hand clothing treasures are to be found, if you're willing to look a little deeper.

Marche de la Creation, 14th arrondissement – This is the city's largest art market, is held on Sundays from 10 am to 7 pm, and here you'll find the most delightful home trinkets you'll ever see, anywhere in Paris.

Galeries Lafayette, 9th arrondissement – Yes, we know what we said about department stores BUT this is Paris' most famous, so even just an hour here will be very rewarding. Besides, the building itself is an absolute stunner, and you must step inside to admire the stained-glass dome roof! Do note that this store is closed on Sundays.

Chapter 8: Best Day Spas in Paris

Parisian women certainly know how to treat themselves, with the city home to a plethora of sublime spa and wellness centers. Whether you're busting for a massage, r wish to indulge in a facial, manicure and pedicure combo, you'll certainly find the right spot for you.

Here are some of the best spas in the city, all of which offer a myriad of treatments for your face and body.

Aquamoon Spa, 1st **arrondissement** – This exquisite spa boasts one of the most gorgeous looking spa baths you'll ever see. With a sauna, hammam and wide array of treatments, Aquamoon is revered for its top notch services, stunning décor, central location and reasonable prices. Can't beat that!

Six Senses, 1st **arrondissement** – On Rue de Castiglione is where you'll find this delightful haven, whose body polishes are nothing short of life-changing. Seriously, silky smooth skin has never felt this good! If you're suffering from a serious case of the jetlag, note that they have a rejuvenating package just for you.

O'Kari Hammam, 2nd **arrondisssement** – Suffering a rainy morning in Paris? Then head to O'Kari after breakfast and there'll be no need to emerge for a few hours. The combo of striking building, excellent services and blissful surroundings make this an ideal R&R spot, most especially on your last day in Paris.

Private Spa Nuxe, 8th arrondissement – Within the prestigious Hotel Le Mathurin, the Private Spa Nuxe is usually only discovered by hotel guests, yet is a worthwhile spa to seek out even if not staying here. With a whirlpool and Turkish bath, this elegant spa offers amazing massages, facials and a host of body treatments. Considering hotel accommodation packages can include treatments and access to the spa, it's a great incentive to stay here.

Spa Le Bristol, 8th arrondissement – The beautiful outdoor terrace with sweeping city views is reason enough to have something, *anything*, done here. One of Paris' most rated spas, Le Bristol is worth its weight in gold. With a comprehensive treatment menu, spa and fitness equipment, you can work out *and* be pampered to your heart's delight. Most beloved for their couple packages, Le Bristol is a heavenly retreat for the woman who's shopped 'till she dropped…and needs a luxurious pick-me-up.

L'Echappee, 11th arrondissement – With glorious treatments, yoga and pilates classes, hammam and massages, there's nothing this superlative spa can't offer. Do note that this place gets jam packed with stressed-out locals on weekends, but is blissfully quiet on weekdays.

Massage Concept Paris, – 1st **arrondissement –** The relaxing atmosphere of central spa is one of its assets, along with a long line of very professional masseuse. After a full week of walking along Paris' streets, you could do no better than a deep tissue massage here.

The ultimate, luxurious splurge…

Institut Dior @ the Hotel Plaza Athenee

What do you get you combine Paris' best known international designer and its foremost luxury hotel? The most opulent spa in the city! Sure a treatment here may set you back a small fortune but to just have the opportunity to try it, once in life, must be heavenly!

Chapter 9: Paris by Night

No matter how tired you're bound to be, after a full day out exploring, chances are you'll want to experience the best of Paris-after-dark. So you should! This gorgeous city is as vibrant after sunset as it is during the day, offering an array of fun and entertaining activities. Plus, Paris at night is purely breathtaking.

Here are some cool things to see and do in Paris of an evening.

It's party time

Paris is awash with trendy bars and nightclubs, but note that the emphasis here is very much on the 'trendy'. Strict dress codes and selective entrance selection affects almost all clubs, irrespective of whether or not they charge an entrance fee. As a woman traveler, however, you'll likely have very few issues with this at all, as bouncers' main prerogative is to ensure there are always more women than men. TimeOut's <u>nightlife guide</u> is a great and constantly updated resource, where you can find the latest and hottest clubs. In a city where clubs open and close at the drop of a beret, it pays to research the best places when *you* intend to visit. Here, you'll find the latest live music and dance bars around.

Generally speaking, however, it's worth keeping in mind that certain areas of Paris tend to attract a certain crowd. In the Latin Quarter, for example, you'll come across clubs frequented by 20-something salsa dancers, whilst around the Champs Elysees you'll find, perhaps unsurprisingly, the most exclusive (and most expensive) clubs in Paris. Le Maris is pure funk and also where most of the city's gay bars are found.

See the Tour Eiffel at night

The spectacular light show, on and emitting from the Eiffel tower is one of the hotly-contested topics among Parisians. Locals hate it and find it abominable that anything so 'tacky' could be taking place in their beloved city. *Everyone else*, however, loves it to bits. Call us kitsch, but we think seeing the Eiffel Tower at night, all lit up like a Christmas tree, is one of the most unforgettable sights you could ever hope to enjoy. For the best views, take the Metro to Trocadero and find the viewing platform close to the Palace of Justice. Magical spot!

Take an evening tour

The Eiffel Tower is not the only attraction illuminated by a sea of lights at night. In fact, the whole city centre literally comes alive after dark, granting it a most enticing ambience. Fat Tire Bike Tours are renowned the world over for their excellent city tours, yet their nightly explorations of Paris, on two wheels, are rated as one of the very best. Spend an evening meandering your way to and past some of the city's most iconic sights, and see just how spellbinding Paris can really be. A totally different way to spend your evening and a most unforgettable addition to any Paris trip.

Catch a Cabaret show

Paris is as synonymous with cabaret shows as it is with croissants, and even if you're a solo woman traveler, you really shouldn't miss catching at least one show when visiting. Cabarets are fun, sensual, mesmerizing, and unlike anything you've ever seen before. Bare breasts and plenty of cheek make cabarets risqué yet classy and very entertaining. It should be noted that all the cabaret clubs nowadays cater for a tourist audience, include English-speaking comedians and many acts which are more 'variety show' rather than traditional cabaret, per se. Nevertheless, this art was still a huge part of Parisian history and experiencing it, at least once, is not something anyone would ever regret.

Most venues in Paris will offer a few options, whether it be full dinner and show, glass of champagne with show, or just show. If travelling alone you may want to skip the dinner part (as this is mostly set up in kitsch tables for two – for added romance!) but definitely opt for a glass of bubbly with your show!

All the clubs mentioned below are renowned for their professional dancers and their high level of skill and entertainment value.

Following are the top three:

The Moulin Rouge, 18th **arrondissement** - Without a doubt, the most famous cabaret venue in the world, the 'Red Windmill' is one of Paris' most iconic sights and the shows, here, attracts crowds like no other. Touristy? Sure! But for damn good reasons; the can-can ending being one of many!

Le Crazy Horse, 8th **arrondissement** – Trailing just a step behind the Moulin Rouge – in popularity - is The Crazy Horse, renowned for its exotic, almost all-nude shows. If you'd like something a little spicier, then this may be for you.

Paradis Latin, 5ᵗʰ arrondissement – This is the oldest cabaret building in the world, built and designed by Gustave Eiffel in 1887, and long listed as a priceless heritage site. Come and watch a phenomenal variety show here and you can soak up the history and the entertainment, all in the one, unforgettable night.

Take an evening cruise own the Seine

Even if you've taken a cruise down the Seine during the day, you really ought to do it all again...at night! Sunset is about the best time, so you can see the glorious golden hues over the Louvre pyramid, Notre Dame and the myriad of other stunning buildings on the Left Bank. Vedettes run about the best night tours of all, with an open-top deck boat and live commentary adding to the fun and amazing views. For the evening cruises, these guys run the best value-for-money tours, with added discounts when tix are bought online. Just skip the dinner. Food is 'just fine' at best and you really need not have your attention of the view disrupted in any way. Have dinner elsewhere before or after your cruise, and enjoy it fully from atop the open deck.

Chapter 10: Useful References

Having the best resources at your fingertips will help you greatly in organizing yoru trip. Aside the handy links we've included thus far, here are some more great websites and links to downloadable maps, whch you should find of use.

ParisInfo: the city's official tourism website

Metro map & RER map: get an overview of the railway system in Paris and keep these maps with you at all times.

SNCF: handy route planner. Simply pop in your location and desired destination and the official public transport system map will show you all the transport options available.

AirBnB: for self-catering options, check out the rooms, apartments and villas available on AirBnB.

Booking.com: comprehensive list of Paris' most popular lodging options

Girls Guide to Paris: constantly updated website aimed at the female traveler

Taxi fare estimator : know roughly how much you *should* be paying to get from A to B

<u>Metro Bar Hop</u> – This fantastic downloadable map highlights the best bars within a short walking distance to each and every Metro stop in Paris. Ideal for those who want to go out exploring after dark...but not too far from the comfort and safety of a Metro stop.

PREVIEW OTHER BOOKS BY THIS AUTHOR

FLORENCE FOR WOMEN: THE ULTIMATE TRAVEL GUIDE FOR WOMEN

by Erica Stewart

[Excerpt from the first 2 Chapters – for complete book, please purchase on Amazon.com]

History and Culture

Any Florence travel guide can never be complete without detailing its rich history and culture. Our guide might specifically cater to our female readers, but it's still important to understand the area's history and culture, isn't it?

The history of Florence can be traced all the way back to the Etruscan times. The city was then known as Fiesole, one that dominated the entire region and was one of the most important Etruscan centers. As the Romans prepared for their war against Fiesole, they set up camp by the Arno River in the 1ˢᵗ century BC. This area was later called Florentia, which can roughly be translated to "destined to flower". Florence somehow managed to survive the Middle Ages as well, and soon became one of the most important cities on the planet.

Florence's growth suffered a major setback because of a dispute between the Ghibellines, those loyal to Emperor Frederick II, and the Guelfs, those loyal to the pope. This led to the Guelfs being exiled from the city, but their absence was apparently short-lived, for they took over Florence once the Emperor succumbed to his death. Despite all the political turmoil, great attention was paid to arts and architecture, and this is one of the main reasons why Florence stands like a shining architectural jewel and a stark reminder of the romantic architectural wonders of a bygone era.

Art and culture were integral to the way of life as well. The desire of its locals to educate themselves led to the birth of the first works in the vernacular language in the form of "Dolce stil novo". This later inspired countless artists such as Boccaccio, Dante and Petrarca as well. In fact, Boccaccio's documentation of the Florence plague is one of the most accurate descriptions of a tragedy that began as dissatisfaction and ended with the "Tumulto dei Ciompi" in the year 1378.

Florence saw a small period where the people took over the rule of the city. However, this was evidently short-lived as the Medici dynasty soon took over. The Medici emperor Lorenzo il Magnifico was also responsible for much of the city's wonderful Brunelleschi architecture. After his death in the year 1492, the city once again fell into turmoil, but this era of conflict still managed to see the rise of world famous artists such as Leonardo da Vinci and Michelangelo.

From the 18th century up until the very beginning of the 20th century, Florence remained famous for its literary offerings and artistic wonders. It produced some of the best works of literature created by writers such as Palazzeschi, Papini and Pratolini, all of whom were members of the literary group "Giubbe Rosse".

Getting There and Around

Florence is well-connected to the rest of Europe and is easy to get into. It has witnessed a drastic increase in tourism over the past few years, and this has led to the development of all sorts of high-tech facilities and traveler-friendly infrastructure.

Getting There

The best way to travel to Florence is by air. The Aeroporto Firenze-Peretola is the main airport of Florence and is located at a distance of 2.5 miles from the city center. The ideal way to commute from the airport is to board the shuttle bus which connects the airport to the Santa Maria Novella station and runs at intervals of 30 minutes between 06.00AM and 11.40PM. Taxi services are available as well.

Getting Around

It makes sense to leave your cars behind while traveling to Florence. And even if you're coming from a faraway destination, forget all about that car rental. As women, one of our main concerns is our security, particularly when traveling to different countries. However, when it comes to Florence, you really don't need a car for most of its major attractions are located in its historic city center, an area best explored on foot (vehicles aren't allowed to enter the city center without prior authorization either). And visiting other destinations is easy as well, for Florence boasts of a decent public transportation system that lets you get from point A to point B without much fuss.

I recommend using the taxi services while in the city, particularly if you're traveling alone. Florence taxis are white in color and can be picked up from a taxi rank or be booked on the phone. Taxi ranks can easily be found in front of the main plazas and railway stations. Some of the top taxi operators in Florence include SO.CO.TA (+39 055 4242) and CO.TA.FI (+39 055 4390).

Florence is relatively small, and this means that a woman can really have a blast while exploring its streets on a bike. There are a number of cycle tracks in the city as well, and this certainly makes things easier. Some of the top bike rental companies to hire your bikes from include Alinari (+39 055 280500), Rentway (+333 9619820), and Florence by bike (+39 055 488992).

For women who like to keep it adventurous, the Segway offers a fascinating option of getting from one place to the other. It's convenient, it's simple and it's certainly super exciting. You can book your Segways by calling +39 055 2398855.

Finally, it is very hard to resist the romantic feel of riding in an open carriage. These enchanting rides transport you to a bygone era and Florence's enchanting cobblestone streets offer the perfect backdrop to relive yesterday. You can easily pick up a carriage in Piazza San Giovanni, Piazza Duomo and Piazza della Signoria.

Staying in Florence

Florence is one of the top cities in Italy for any woman wanting to choose from a wide range of safe, secure, exciting and inviting accommodations. Florence was among the first cities in Italy to develop its hotel scene, particularly because of the efforts of local designer Michele Bonan, who has now left his mark on hotels across the country, and the hospitality division of the Ferragamo Group, Lungarno Hotels.

Hotels for Every Budget

The city has always enjoyed a great tradition of hospitality and she takes a lot of pride in introducing her female travelers to some of its best-kept secrets. There's a lot of choice across all budgets, even in the historic city center, the place where you really want to be. Better yet, the competition amongst hotels keeps rates at a low, particularly during the off season.

For Ladies Wanting to Live like Locals

If you're dreaming of staying in an area that is full of artisan workshops, real people and hidden cafes, look no further than the Oltrarano district. Some of the top accommodation options include the cute B&B Floroom 1 and the Palazzo Magnani Feroni.

Billed as one of the top bed and breakfasts in the city, **B&B Floroom 1** is a sleek address located on the banks of the Arno River, and one of the top choices for solo female travelers looking for budgeted options in the city. This four-bedroom B&B boasts of an extremely relaxed atmosphere and each of its four rooms feature wooden floors, white walls, rustic ceilings and giant photographs of Florence. The old-new combination works quite well and really makes the property stand out. Some rooms also boast of four-poster beds, and an opaque glass wall hides away the comfy bathroom that has been fitted with pewter fittings and rainforest showerheads.

The **Palazzo Magnani Feroni** is one hotel that you'd never want to leave. It makes you feel like the nobility of yesterday and transports you to a historic location that makes you forget about everything else. Each aristocratic suite boasts of beautiful high curved ceilings and heirloom furniture and the terrace views rank among the very best.

For the Budget-Conscious Woman (Medium Range)

Casa Di Barbano is a simple option that offers great value for money. It is spacious and elegant and its owners are extremely friendly. All rooms are comfortable to say the least, and when you factor in the convenient location, safe accommodations, and reasonable costs, you have everything you need to explore Florence like a pro.

Casa Nuestra is one of the hippest addresses in the city. This brand new B&B is located close to the Campo di Marti station, and is characterized by its super friendly hosts. Apart from offering picture-perfect accommodations, the owners also go out of their way to assist you in planning your itineraries, show you how to explore the city and help you uncover enchanting walking paths.

For the Lady Who Travels in Style.... (Luxury)

Palazzo Vecchietti is one of the most elegant and beautiful hotels in the city. This boutique hotel boasts of stylish rooms, easy access to Via Tornabuoni and a superior level of service. The furnishings have been tastefully appointed, and great attention has been paid to every detail. Beds are comfy and usually include quality beddings and cashmere blankets. They are the just about the perfect places to snuggle into after a long and tiring day exploring the artistic wonders around the city.

Another popular option is the *St. Regis Hotel*. It boasts of a unique ambience that is both delightful and discreet at the same time. The hotel is located on an enchanting riverside location in centro storico and its Arno views appeals to female travelers who are accustomed to the highest standards of pampering. The service is warm and welcoming, professional and casual, discreet and attentive. Everything you'd want it to be. And the rooms are just what you'd expect from a hotel like St. Regis. I would recommend the Bottega Veneta suite, a top option for fashion-conscious women.

Things to See and Do

No matter how many times you come to visit this iconic beauty, you won't be able to see it all. A bridge on the Arno River is one of the first destinations that you should visit while in Florence. It is known to offer different experiences at different times of the day, for the views, the light, and the atmosphere changes each and every time. Considered to be the birthplace of the Renaissance, Florence also boasts of some of the best art and architecture in history. No wonder it manages to draw millions of tourists year after year.

Walking in the Footsteps of Michelangelo

Very few artists have managed to leave their mark on a city the way Michelangelo has in Florence. The city is home to some of his greatest masterpieces, and one of the biggest charms of visiting the city is to retrace his steps and explore places that are linked to his memories. Embarking on the following itinerary not only lets you retrace Michelangelo's steps, but also brings you closer to some of the most important arts and monuments in Florence. Remember, the ideal way to make the most of this itinerary is to spread it over two days, so that you get enough time to marvel at the various wonders and enjoy all that it has in store for you.

Start off your explorations at the **Casa Buonarroti**. Located in the vibrant Santa Croce, Casa Buonarroti is the palace where the artist's family lived. It was built by his nephew Leonardo, and passed hands from one member of the family to another until the iconic family finally became extinct. Casa Buonarroti hosts some of the earliest works of Michelangelo such as the *Madonna della Scala* and the *Battle of the Centaurs*. The former is a tribute to sculptor Donatello while the latter has been inspired by the Garden of San Marco. Both masterpieces were created by the artist while he was in his twenties, and imagining a young boy creating such outstanding works of art is an exciting experience in itself.

The next destination is the **Church of Santo Spirito**, another place that has been intricately linked with Michelangelo during his early days. Located in the Oltrarno district, the church is considered to be one of the most beautiful Renaissance-era churches on the planet. It was also the place where Michelangelo found accommodation after his patron Lorenzo de Medici died in the year 1492. The church is famous for its inspiring wooden *Crucifix* that Michelangelo created in the year 1493.

The next step of your journey takes you to the **Bargello Museum**. Michelangelo was forced to move to Rome in the year 1494 after the city riots sent Medici into exile, and it was in Rome that he created the world famous *Bacchus*, now located in the Bargello Museum. The museum is also home to other popular artworks created by the artist such as *David/ Apollo, Brutus,* and *Tondo Pitti.*

Don't forget to add the **Accademia Gallery** into your itinerary as well. Once Michelangelo returned to Florence in the year 1501, he set about creating some of his best works of art, including the outstanding *David*, now located in the Accademia Gallery. The Accademia is also home to many of his unfinished figures and sculptures. From the "*non finito*" sculpting techniques of *St. Mathew* to the marble wonder *Prigioni*, the Accademia truly showcases some of the most the distinct features of Michelangelo's style.

Head over to the **Uffizi Art Gallery** next. Considered to be one of the most famous art galleries in the world, Uffizi features a large collection of artworks created between the 12th and 17th centuries by leading artists such as Leonardo da Vinci, Botticelli, Raffaello and

Giotto. The gallery also houses the *Tondo Doni*, Michelangelo's first canvas painting and the only of its kind in Florence.

Between the years 1515 and 1534, the Medici family saw two of its members becoming popes – Clement VIII and Leo X. Michelangelo was commissioned to create the *Laurentian Library* for the *Basilica of San Lorenzo* and the *Sagrestia Nuova* for the **Medici Chapels**. Both works of art are a must see and the entire complex is also worth a visit for its artistic ingenuity.

The last Michelangelo masterpiece that you should admire during your stay in Florence is the *Pieta Bandini*. This dramatic work of art was created in the year 1550 and is now located in the **Museo dell'Opera del Duomo**. It is considered to be one of the greatest examples of the master's work and what makes it even more special is his self-portrait, a male figure flanked by Mary and Magdalene, holding the lifeless body of Christ.

Best Neighborhoods

When planning any vacation, one of the biggest concerns for women is to choose the right neighborhood. There are some areas that have traditionally been famous for being safe for women, while ensuring that they don't miss out on the very best of nightlife and cosmopolitan delights that the city has to offer. When it comes to Florence, you need to decide between three choices – staying in the historic center, staying outside of the historic center or staying in the surrounding countryside. All three areas have safe neighborhoods for women, so it ultimately boils down to personal preference. Here are a few options to choose from.

Staying Within the Historic Center

The city center always dominates a major part of your holiday for most of the historic sights and attractions are located here. The area is among the oldest parts of the city, and the ring that you see is basically the spot where those 13th century walls were built. The city center is quite small, and car free as well. This means that you can easily walk from one place to the other and not miss a car throughout your journey. Staying close to the Santa Maria Novella station puts you within a 5-minute walk from the Duomo and staying close to the Duomo pits you within a 5-minute walk from Ponte Vecchio and Palazzo Vecchio. The ideal way to choose an area is to look for accommodations close to the sites you really like. Since most of the major sites are quite close to each other, I suggest staying between Piazza Santa Croce, Piazza San Marco, Piazza Santa Maria Novella and Pont Vecchio. This area is among the busiest areas in the city and is always full of tourists all through the day and in the evenings as well. The second option is to look for accommodations in the Oltrarno neighborhood, but that only works if you're leaning towards local experiences, unique furniture galleries and the Pitti Palace.

Staying Outside the Historic Center

With most of the restaurants, cafes, sights and attractions located within the historic center, you would argue if it makes sense to stay outside the center. However, many female travelers visiting Florence end up booking accommodations outside its historic center for all sorts of reasons. The biggest advantage of staying outside the city center is that it is friendlier on the wallet. Moreover, anyone wanting to stay in a residential area to explore the local way of life needs to step outside the touristic city center. A few areas that aren't really far from the main sights of the city include Via Bolognese, Fortezza da Basso, Poggio Imperiale and Piazza Beccaria.

Staying in the Surrounding Countryside

If you're thinking of keeping Florence as a base for exploring Tuscany, you might want to head over to the surrounding hills. Apart from letting you get up close and personal to nature, it also lets you enjoy all sorts of amenities such as gardens, outdoor areas and swimming pools in your accommodations without forcing you to pay through the roof. Having your own rental car is a must while staying in the outskirts, but it's perfect for exploring Tuscany to its fullest.

[Excerpt from the first 2 Chapters – for complete book, please purchase on Amazon.com]

Made in the USA
Coppell, TX
24 November 2020

41984768R00046